"*AMERICAN TELEVISION* is a radical deconstruction of all that is red, white, and blue. J.I.B. takes the American myth and pulls you behind its curtain to show you the machination of empire and class— crafting a scathing rebuttal of patriotism and the elite. *AMERICAN TELEVISION* is the doomer manifesto — a guide to new radical thought."

   -Damian Rucci, author of *Last of the Hard Core*

"*AMERICAN TELEVISION* is the rotting abscess in the gleaming teeth of a television cowboy.It is a fever dream of talkshows and live footage of the next war, and the war after that. It praises the ammunition and passes the lord. *AMERICAN TELEVISION* is an invocation, a curse, invective and praise.Buy American"

   -Jacob Rakovan author of "*The Devil's Radio*" and "*Ars Memoria*"

AMERICAN TELEVISION

Poems by JIB

Spartan
Press

Spartan Press

Kansas City, Missouri

spartanpresskc.com

Spartan
Press

Acknowledgments

"America and the Truth" was published by *Rust Belt Press* in April of 2022.

"Comprehensive History of Portsmouth, Ohio" was published in the Spring 2022 edition of *Main Street Rag*.

"What it Means to be an American, a Personal Essay" was accepted by *Big Windows Review* in October of 2021.

"Matt Lauer, 2005/ Why I Learned to Stop Sleeping" was accepted by *ilanot journal* in November of 2021.

"A Beaten Dog…", "Everything Collected…" and "The Part of the Brain…" were all included in *"This is Not a Song"*, a chapbook published by *Toast Boy* in November of 2023.

"Theories on Car Wrecks and Other Forms of Suicide", "Chris Watts Had a Problem", "Me and Louie Anderson…" and "Brenda Ann Spencer/ A Ruger 10/22, Semi Automatic" "Lonliness and VHS Thecnologies", were included in *"Our Tiny Little Lives"*, published by Alienbuddha Press in October of 2021.

"Charlie Mason…", "Talk Shows and G.G. ALin's War on America…", "Sinkholes in America", "Norman Rockwell…" were featured in the anthology *"Not Ready for the River Styx"*, published by Back of the Class Press in 2023.

Table of Contents

A Lot of Mess and American Television / 1

What it Means to be an American, a
     Personal Essay / 20

America and the Truth / 21

A Comprehensive History of Portsmouth,
     Ohio / 22

Sinkholes in America / 24

Theories on CAr Wrecks and Other Forms
     of Suicide / 26

Me and Louie Anderson, Autumn of 1999 / 28

Matt Lauer, 2005/ Why I Learned to Stop
     Sleeping / 30

A Beaten Dog/C-PTSD / 31

Everything Collected Turns to Rage / 32

My Step Father Taught my Brother to Aim / 33

Loneliness and the Resurgence of VHS
     Technologies / 34

Norman Rockwell and a World that Never
     Existed / 35

Use Dynamite as Required / 37

The Stability/Instability Paradox / 38

Chris Watts had a Problem / 40

Brenda Ann Spencer/ A Ruger 10/22, Semi
     Automatic / 41

A Short List of People I'm Trying
     to Kill / 43

American Culture and Its
        Consequences / 47
Talk Shows and G.G. Allin's War
        on America, 1956-1993 / 48
Charlie Manson and Violence and
        the United States' Prison
        Industrial Complex and How
        They Correlate / 52
The Part of the Brain that Forms
        Society and The Part of the
        Brain That Designs and Sets
        Traps / 54
American Youth, The Early 21st
        Century / 58
A Hammering and the Hole it Made / 60
The Suncoast Digest with Christine
Chubbuck/Performance Art and American
        Television / 62
American Television and Unanswered
        Questions / 64

This book is dedicated to America and Americans. To apple pie. To Uncle Sam. To Fat Man and to Little Boy. To the horse they rode in on. To J. Robert Oppenhimer. To God. To J. Edgar Hoover. To John Wayne. To Pogo the Clown. To Marsilio Ficino. To Diogenes. To Jean-Michel Basquiat. To Jerry Springer. To Jesus on the cross. To failing infrastructure. To Bert the Turtle. To Bjork. To dynamite and other forms of explosives. To John Brown. To Adolf. To Norman Rockwell. To Charlie Manson. To G.G Allin. To Christine Chubbuck. To Martin Scorsese. To Francis Ford Coppola. To Harvey Pekar. To MF DOOM. To blood and guts. To the unbearable pressure. To Dan Denton. To Ezhno Martin. To Jason Ryberg. To burning buildings. To the prison industrial complex. To cancerous tumors. To beaten dogs. To the ones who beat them. To the glorification of war. To the importance of icons. To martyrs and martyrdom. To Aaron Bushnell. To Aaron Bushnell. To Aaron Bushnell. To the victims of George Washington's teeth. To Ron and Nancy. To John Hickley Jr. To Quentin Tarantino. To the distinction between sex and violence. To the artist who designed the gun. To Martin Shkreli. To Anish Kapoor. To Jim Irsay. To Ted Turner. To being lied to. To manifestos and the author of manifestos. To fucking what you hate and killing what you love and hating what you fuck and loving what you kill. To any and all icons who helped shape America. To the beautiful people and to the murders. To the murderers of the beautiful people. To the unbearable pressure. To unanswered questions. To American television.

"You shouldn't let poets lie to you"

-Bjork

AMERICAN TELEVISION

A Lot of Mess and American Television

"I remember being very scared because an Icelandic poet told me that not like in cinemas, where the (projector) just sends light on the screen, this is different. This is millions and millions of little screens that send light… But because there are so many of them, and in fact you are watching very many things when you are watching TV, your head is very busy all the time to calculate and put it all together into one picture. And then because you're so busy doing that, you don't watch very carefully what the program you are watching is really about. So you become hypnotized. So all that's on TV, it just goes directly into your brain and you stop judging if it's right or not. You just swallow and swallow. This is what an Icelandic poet told me." — Bjork, Icelandic pop star, on the nature of television

Millions of little lights.

CONSUME.

WHAT ELSE?

AMERICA.

Drilling millions of little holes.

AMERICAN TELEVISION.

AMERICAN TELEVISION.

AMERICAN

TELEVISION.

Fucking and hating
and falling in love.
A woman eating a
hamburger in a bikini
on a hot car. A summer
day. A lot of swallowing.

AMERICAN TELEVISION,
BREAKING
NEWS. sex/power/violence.

Alexander the Great wept.

Killing
What you
love and

The things America understand.

BEAUTIFUL

Filling in the
hole. Filling in the hole.

PEOPLE.

sex/power/violence.RADICALIZED. A Product of my environment.

fucking
what you

What else?

History made every 24 hours. Network news.
A major war every 20 years
and a big budget motion picture.

Hating and hating.

(THE SOUND OF A HOLE BEING DRILLED)

Hating and hating and loving.

Hate.

(THE SOUND OF A HOLE BEING DRILLED)
(THE SOUND OF A HOLE BEING DRILLED)

There is no more World Left.

CONSUME. WHAT ELSE?

STAY TUNED. BEING LIED TO.
SWALLOW. ALWAYS.
BEAUTIFUL
PEOPLE. BEAUTIFUL
PEOPLE
PEOPLE. More holes.

CONSUME. WHAT ELSE? **STAY TUNED.**

BEAUTIFUL. BEAUTIFUL. PEOPLE. KILLING. HATING.

The computers can only swallow and vomit.

A head very busy. A lot of mess.
Confusion.

LOVING. HATING. LOVING. HATING. LOVING. KILLING.
HATING. LOVING. KILLING. EATING. WHAT ELSE. **AMERICAN
TELEVISION.**
PEOPLE.   **KILL/FUCK/EAT/LOVE/HATE.**
RADICALIZED.

And the unanswered questions.

CONSUME. WHAT ELSE?

ARMY STRONG. (Gun fire. Canned laughter)

A LOT OF FIRING GUNS.

Confusion. CONSUME.

SEX/VIOLENCE/POWER

KILL/FUCK/EAT/LOVE/HATE.

There's nothing else.
CONSUME. NEVER CONSIDER.
CONSUME. NEVER CONSIDER.
RIGHT OR NOT. CONSUME. STAY
TUNED. NEVER CONSIDER. RIGHT
OR NOT. NEVER CONSIDER. RIGHT
OR NOT. NEVER. **RADICALIZED.**

CONSUME. WHAT ELSE? A LOT OF

PRETENDING.   More holes.   And why won't the
hammering stop? And why won't the hammering
stop?

Over a million died in the making *Apocalypse
NOW.*   CONSUME.

   CONSUME. Nearly 200,000 people were burned to
DEATH by the ATOMIC BOMB.

  WHAT ELSE? AMERICA. A LOT OF PRETENDING.
There's nothing else.
CONSUME. **FLAME BROILED MEAT. OVER A
BILLION SERVED (IN COUNTING)** WHAT

ELSE? AMERICA. Directed by Christopher Nolan.
 sex/power/violence. **BEING LIED TO**

   WHAT ELSE? AMERICA. sex/power/violence. AMERICA.
(SELLING BURGERS AND CARS AND GOD)

     AND THE HAMMERING NEVER STOPS. HAMMERING NEVER
STOPS. AND THE HAMMERING. HAMMERING NEVER

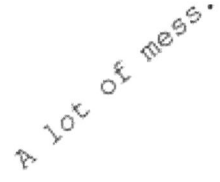
A lot of mess.

A child and American television and nothing
else but swallowing. And swallowing and
vomiting and swallowing again and
swallowing and vomiting and swallowing
again and swallowing and vomiting and
swallowing again and hating what you fuck
and killing what you love and fucking what
you hate and loving what you kill and
confusion and mess and nothing else.

American Television.

STOPS.HAMMERING NEVER STOPS. **AMERICAN TELEVISION.**
AND THE HAMMERING. AND THE HAMMERING.
(Seen not represented) Laughing and crying
and smiling without meaning it. Screaming.
Laughing. Loving. Hating. Killing.
Fucking. Loving. Killing. Smiling. Not
meaning it.

     Directed by Francis Ford Coppola. **I'M A**

PRODUCT OF MY ENVIRONMENT.
KILL/FUCK/EAT/LOVE/HATE. Filling in a
hole. Repeating what they see and believing what
they're told. Repeating what they see and
believing what they're told. Repeating what they
see and believing what they're told.
Repeating what they see and believing what they're
told.
(The credits roll)   **RADICALIZED.**
RADICALIZED.   **RADICALIZED.**
 Filling in a hole. Beautiful people murdering and
being murdered and murdering and being murdered
and murdering and being murdered. (Now a word from
your sponsor)   (IT"S 10PM. DO you know where
your children are?)   And why won't the hammering
stop?

(INTRO THEME PLAYS)   **CONSUME. WHAT ELSE?**

Filling in a hole. Filling in a hole. More holes.
More holes. THIS IS YOUR BRAIN ON DRUGS.
     CONSUME. WHAT ELSE? CONSUME. WHAT
ELSE? BREAKING NEWS.
   A child and American television and nothing else but swallowing. And
     swallowing and vomiting and swallowing again and swallowing
     and vomiting and swallowing
        again and swallowing and vomiting and swallowing.
    THERE IS ALWAYS GOING TO BE
    AMERICAN TELEVISION.

    BLOOD AND GUTS. AMERICAN TELEVISION. **A WAR.** AMERICAN TELEVISION.
(THE SOUND OF A HOLE BEING DRILLED) BLOOD AND GUTS AND FALLING IN LOVE.
  (THE SOUND OF A HOLE BEING DRILLED) **And the unanswered questions.**

Hating what you fuck and killing what you love and fucking what you hate and loving what you kill   and confusion   and mess and nothing else.
STARRING MARLON BRANDO. STARRING MARTIN SHEEN. AMERICAN TELEVISION.
RADICALIZED.

American Television. American television. **The glorification of war. The glorification of war.**
American   (INTRO THEME PLAYS)
          (SELLING BURGERS AND MEDICINE AND GOD)   **The glorification of war. The glorification of war.**   television. Stay tuned. BREAKING
BREAKING NEWS.   BREAKING.
               The glorification of war. AMERICAN TELEVISION.
NEWS. More holes.   And why won't the hammering stop?
RADICALIZED.   **CONSUME. WHAT ELSE?** Filling in the hole.
THERE'S GOING TO BE A WAR.
               There's always going to be a war. **THERE'S GOING TO BE**
                                        A WAR. What else?
CONSUME. WHAT ELSE? CONSUME. WHAT ELSE? FUCKING AND HATING AND
          KILLING AND EATING AND LAUGHING   There's no more
World Left.
          AND FALLING IN LOVE. **AND THE HAMMERING.** (Now a word
from your sponsor)
RADICALIZED.
          (The Sound of a drill. Canned laughter. Roll
credit.)   BEAUTIFUL
     RADICALIZED.

RADICALIZED.

PEOPLE.   PEOPLE.   Scared.
People. RADICALIZED.

     Scared. PEOPLE.

RADICALIZED. RADICALIZED.

RADICALIZED.   Scared people
radicalized. **RADICALIZED.**

Scared people. **RADICALIZED.** What

else?
(the commodification of necessity and joy) (the
commodification of necessity and joy) (the
commodification of necessity and joy) (the
commodification of necessity and joy)
Always drilling and filling. Always drilling and

filling. Always drilling and filling. Always
drilling and filling. Always drilling and filling.

ALexander the Great wept.   FUCk WITH THE LIGHTS
OFF/

KILL IN PUBLIC

THIS IS YOUR BRAIN ON DRUGS.   THIS IS YOUR
BRAIN ON DRUGS.

What do you do with the unbearable
pressure?

(The visible invisible) **A child. Laughing
at jokes he doesn't understand. A
child.**   **A child. Laughing at jokes he
doesn't understand. A child.** A product of
my environment. What else? (the
commodification of necessity and joy)

AND WHAT DOES IT MEAN TO LOVE?   **And the
unanswered questions. And the unanswered
questions.**

And the glorification of war. And the
glorification of war.

THERE IS GOING TO BE A WAR. (INTRO THEME PLAYS)
AND THE HAMMERING NEVER STOPS. STAY TUNED.

(CANNED LAUGHTER. A CHILD'S
SCREAM.)

HISTORY MADE EVERY 24 HOURS.
STAY TUNED.
ONE PICTURE. ONE PICTURE. ONE
PICTURE. NEVER
sex/power/violence. CONSIDER
RIGHT OR NOT. ONE PICTURE. 3,000
Americans burn alive. TELEVISED.
Being very scared.
RADICALIZED. sex/power/violenc.
sex/power/violence.
sex/power/violence. sex/power/violen.
**BEING VERY SCARED. AN
UNBEARABLE   PRESSURE.** A

LOT OF PRETENDING. AMERICAN TELEVISION.

A LOT OF SMILING. RADICALIZED. More holes. (The visible invisible)

DR.PHIL: *When You had your hands around her throat, and you were choking her, what did you want to happen? DID YOU WANT HER TO DIE?* DR.PHIL: *Do you love her?* A LOT OF FIRING GUNS. sex/power/violence. sex/power/violence.

KILLING. KILLING. KILLING. AMERICAN TELEVISION. (SELLING BURGERS) **AND BEING LIED TO.** AMERICA. (Selling cars) BREAKING NEWS. BREAKING NEWS.

AND BEING LIED TO. (The credits roll) (Now a word from your sponsor)

Nearly 3,000 people burned to death in New York City. Two skyscrapers ash. Two countries in the Middle East. TELEVISED. Over 7,000 soldiers. DEAD. TELEVISED. **RADICALIZED.** 20 years of this.

Over 30,000 more from suicide after combat. THE HAMMERING NEVER STOPS. Being very scared. Being very scared. Being very scared.

RADICALIZED. BEING VERY SCARED. FUCK WITH THE LIGHTS   (THE SOUND OF A HOLE BEING DRILLED) AMERICAN TELEVISION. OFF.

Being very scared. AND THE HAMMERING. **KILL IN PUBLIC. (GUN FIRE) A LOT OF MESS AND A LOT OF**

Fuck with the lights off/kill in public. Fuck with the lights off/kill in public. Fuck with the lights off/kill in public. Beautiful people murdering and being murdered. Falling in love. Filling in the hole. Filling a hole.

DRILLING A MILLION LITTLE HOLES. (THE SOUND OF A HOLE BEING DRILLED) It's AMERICA. AMERICA. AMERICA.   More holes. Directed by Sam Mendes.

THE FEW THE PROUD THE MARINES. (FADE TO BLACK. ROLL CREDITS)

FUCKING AND HATING AND KILLING AND EATING AND
LAUGHING AND FALLING IN LOVE. **KILL IN PUBLIC.** OVER A
MILLION KILLED IN VIETNAM. TELEVISED.

100,000 people died in the making of
JARHEAD (2005)

CONSUME. WHAT ELSE? **A CHILD AND AMERICAN
TELEVISION.**

Drilling and filling. Drilling and
filling. Drilling and filling.
Drilling and filling. Drilling and
filling. Drilling and filling.

ALWAYS. ALWAYS.

Drilling and **ALWAYS** filling.
Drilling and
filling. Drilling and filling.
Drilling and

Filling and **ALWAYS** drilling and
filling.
Drilling and filling.

RADICALIZED. **RADICALIZED.**

HEAD VERY BUSY. CONSUME. WHAT ELSE? HEAD
VERY BUSY. HEAD VERY BUSY. HEAD VERY BUSY.
AND BEING LIED TO. HEAD VERY BUSY. HEAD
VERY BUSY. sex/power/violence. **FUCK WITH THE
LIGHTS OFF.** It's AMERICA.

HEAD VERY BUSY ALL TIME. ALL
THE TIME HEAD VERY BUSY.

CONSUME. WHAT ELSE? Beautiful
people being murdered. There's no
more world left. It's AMERICA.

SIDE EFFECTS MAY INCLUDE Directed
by Quentin Tarantino. (THE SOUND OF A HOLE
BEING DRILLED). I AM PREPARED FOR COMBAT.
sex/power/violence. Never consider right or not.
It's AMERICA. AMERICA. AMERICA. ONE

PICTURE.   ALWAYS. BEAUTIFUL.
(GUN FIRE). (SELLING CARS AND GOD AND CARS).
More holes.   IT"S AMERICA

And why won't the hammering stop?
(THE SOUND OF A HOLE BEING DRILLED) AMERICA.   PEOPLE FALLING IN LOVE.
I AM A PRODUCt OF MY ENVIRONMENT.   and fucking and THIS IS YOUR BRAIN ON
DRUGS.
And being lied to. And being lied to.

And **being lied to.** A LOT OF MESS AND A LOT OF
CONFUSION. A LOT OF MESS AND A LOT OF KILLING.
Always a good guy and a bad. **And killing.** There's
nothing else.

Something America understands.
RADICALIZED.
I AM PROUD TO BE AN AMERICAN.
Something Americans understand.
Radicalized. Always a good guy and
a bad.
ROUGHLY 12,000,000 dead from
AMERICAN WAR (And Counting)
THERE IS ALWAYS GOING TO BE A WAR. Things
Americans understand.
CONSUME.   (SELLING
BURGERS) What do you do with
the unbearable pressure? 32 shot
dead in Blacksburg Virginia.
(THE SOUND OF GUNFIRE) CONSUME.
WHAT ELSE? **Beautiful**
people murdering.
WHAT ELSE? Being lied to.
CONSUME. WHAT ELSE?
STAY TUNED.   168 dead in
Oklahoma City.   Put it all together.
Put it all   together. THERE'S NO MORE
WORLD LEFT. **AND WHAT DOES IT MEAN**
TO HATE? AND WHAT DOES IT MEAN TO
KILL?
And the unanswered
questions.

CONSUME.   There's nothing else. There's nothing else.   WHAT else? PUT IT ALL TOGETHER. There's nothing else. More holes.

(Now a word from your sponsor)
THIS IS NOT A FULL LIST OF SIDE EFFECTS.
                    Always a showdown at dusk.
THINGS AMERICANS UNDERSTAND.
A child laughing at jokes they don't understand. Filling in the hole. Being very sacred. Being very scared. AMERICAN TELEVISION. A Child. Filling in the hole.

THIS IS YOUR BRAIN ON DRUGS. (The visible invisible)   PUT IT ALL TOGETHER. ONE PICTURE.   PUT IT ALL TOGETHER. AMERICAN TELEVISION.

CONSUME.   Blood and guts and blood and guts and blood and guts.
 WHAT ELSE? CONSUME   WHAT ELSE? Filling in the whole. Filling in the hole. Filling in the hole. Filling in the hole.

Filling in the hole.   THIS IS YOUR BRAIN ON DRUGS.   WHAT DOES THE OUROBOROS EAT WHEN THERE'S NOTHING ELSE?
(the commodification of necessity and joy) (the promotion of hedonism as solution to our problems) Filling a hole. Filling a hole.

CONSUME. Very scared all the time. Very scared.   IT'S AMERICA. IT'S AMERICA.

WHAT ELSE?   The glorification of war. The glorification of war.

The commodification of necessity and
joy. AMERICAN TELEVISION.
ALEXANDER THE GREAT WEPT. There's nothing else.
AMERICAN TELEVISION.

(INTRO THEME PLAYS) There's
always going to be a war. There's always going to
be a war.
 There's always going to be a war. Always a good
guy and a bad. Always a showdown at dawn. There's
always going to be a war.
 There's always going to be a war. RADICALIZED.
PREPARE FOR COMBAT. And why won't the
hammering stop? AND WHAT DOES IT MEAN TO HATE? AND
WHAT DOES IT MEAN TO KILL? AND WHAT DOES IT MEAN TO
HATE? AND WHAT DOES IT MEAN TO KILL? AMERICAN
TELEVISION.

PUT IT ALL TOGETHER. ONE PICTURE.
PUT IT ALL TOGETHER. ONE PICTURE.
PUT IT ALL TOGETHER. ONE PICTURE.
PUT IT ALL TOGETHER. ONE PICTURE.

AMERICAN TELEVISION. **AMERICAN TELEVISION.** AMERICAN
TELEVISION. **(The sound of a drill. The sound
of a child screaming. A gun firing.
Canned laughter. Fade to black. Roll
credits)** Things Americans
understand. PUT IT ALL TOGETHER.

ONE PICTURE. PUT IT ALL
TOGETHER. ONE PICTURE.

Being very scared. Being very scared.
Things Americans understand.
(The visible invisible)
What do you do with the
unbearable pressure? What do you
do with the unbearable pressure?
Killing in public. AMERICA.
Being lied to. Being lied to.
AMERICA. America. Filling in the
hole. Filling in a hole. A
child. A child. A child. A
child. WHAT DOES THE

OUROBOROS EAT WHEN THERE'S NOTHING ELSE?
Being very scared. Just swallowing. Being very scared.
Being very scared. RADICALIZED. A child. Being very scared. Just swallowing. Being very scared. HAMMERING NEVER STOPS. IT'S AMERICA.   CONSUME. Being very scared. **What Else?** Being lied to. Being very scared. Being lied to. Being lied to. Being lied to. Being lied to.
There's nothing else. There's nothing else. There's nothing else.
What do you do with the unbearable pressure?
RADICALIZED. (THE SOUND OF A HOLE BEING DRILLED) **AMERICA.** (THE SOUND OF A HOLE BEING DRILLED) **AMERICA. AND WHAT DOES IT MEAN TO HATE? AND WHAT DOES IT MEAN TO KILL?**
(INTRO THEME PLAYS)   The glorification of war. The glorification of war. **THIS IS YOUR BRAIN ON DRUGS.**
(Now a word from your sponsor)
                  DRILLING MILLIONS OF HOLES.
Directed by   Steven Spielberg.
Directed by Oliver Stone. WHAT DOES THE OUROBOROS EAT WHEN THERE'S NOTHING ELSE? **PUT IT ALL TOGETHER. ONE PICTURE.**

Being very scared. **STARRING TOM HANKS.** It's AMERICA.
(SELLING INSURANCE) WHAT ELSE? IT'S AMERICA. IT'S AMERICA.
Blood and guts and blood and guts. 15 dead in Columbine Colorado. 26 dead in Newtown Connecticut. The glorification of violence. Being very scared. Being very

scared. Being very scared.
Being very scared. A child. A
child. Being very scared.
Being very scared.
The way a child repeats
and believes Being very scared.
what they're told.   THIS
IS YOUR BRAIN ON DRUGS. THIS IS
YOUR BRAIN ON DRUGS.
WHAT ELSE?   CONSUME. WHAT
ELSE? FUCK WITH THE
Never consider right or not. Never considering. Never.
LIGHTS OFF/ KILL ALEXANDER THE GREAT WEPT.
IT'S AMERICA.   IN PUBLIC.
sex/power/violence. sex/power/violence. There's
nothing else. AND WHAT DOES IT MEAN
TO HATE? AND WHAT DOES IT MEAN TO
KILL?
                    There's nothing else.
AND KILLING AND EATING AND LAUGHING AND FALLING IN
LOVE. AND KILLING AND EATING AND
LAUGHING AND FALLING IN LOVE. AND
WHAT DOES IT MEAN TO BE AMERICAN?

Always a good guy and a bad. Always a good guy
and   AND WHAT DOES IT MEAN TO
                              LOVE?
a bad. **Radicalized.** Never consider right or
not. Never consider.
Head very busy. Head very busy. Head
very busy. CONSUME. There's
nothing else. (The visible
invisible)
The dianoise is bleak. Stay stunned.
AMERICA. (The visible invisible) (the
commodification of necessity and
joy) (the promotion of hedonism as
solution to our problems)

Drilling and filling. **AND WHAT DOES IT MEAN TO BE AMERICAN?** Drilling and filling. Drilling and filling and **AMERICAN TELEVISION**.. Drilling and filling.AND DRILLING. AND DRILLING. AND DRILLING. Drilling and filling. Drilling and filling. AND THE HAMMERING. Drilling and filling. **AND WHAT DOES IT MEAN TO BE AMERICAN?**

AND WHAT DOES IT MEAN TO HATE? AND WHAT DOES IT MEAN TO KILL? A LOT OF MESS. sex/power/violence. **AMERICAN TELEVISION. AMERICAN TELEVISION.** WHAT DOES THE OUROBOROS EAT WHEN THERE'S NOTHING ELSE?

G.G ALLIN: *I"ve had sex with men and women and animals.* **AND THE HAMMERING. AND THE HAMMERING.** A LOT OF MESS AND A LOT OF FUKING AND A LOT OF KILLING AND A LOT OF HATING AND A LOT OF FIRING GUNS.

AMERICAN TELEVISION. IT'S AMERICA. IT's AMERICA. THE PRESSURE.
AMERICAN TELEVISION. PUT IT ALL TOGETHER. ONE PICTURE.
History being made every 24 hours.
Prepare. Prepare. Prepare. Prepare.
A child and American television and nothing else but swallowing. **BEING VERY SCARED. AMERICAN TELEVISION.** And swallowing and vomiting and swallowing again and swallowing. I AM A PRODUCT OF MY ENVIRONMENT. I AM A PRODUCT OF MY ENVIRONMENT. I AM A PRODUCT OF MY ENVIRONMENT. **WHAT ELSE? Beautiful PEOPLE.** Always a good guy and a bad. Always a showdown at dawn. **AMERICAN TELEVISION. AMERICAN TELEVISION. AND WHAT DOES IT MEAN TO BE AMERICAN?**

CONSUME. WHAT ELSE? and hating what you fuck and killing what you love and fucking what you hate and loving what you kill and confusion and mess. And confusion and mess. And confusion dn mess and blood and guts. And blood and guts. Blood. Guts. And blood and guts. AMERICAN TELEVISION.
CONSUME. WHAT ELSE? Nothing else. Blood and guts. More holes. AND WHAT DOES IT MEAN TO HATE? AND WHAT DOES IT MEAN TO KILL? NOW I AM BECOME DEATH. A LOT OF MESS.

American Television. There's nothing else. Things Americans understand.

Confused? Things Americans understand. Stay tuned. CONSUME. WHAT ELSE? Things Americans understand. Put it all together and swallow. Put it all together and swallow. What do you do with the unbearable pressure? What do you do with the unbearable pressure? What do you do with unbearable pressure?

FUCK WITH THE LIGHTS OFF/ KILL. NEVER CONSIDER RIGHT OR NOT. **(The visible invisible)**
(Now a word from your sponsor)

IN PUBLIC. **NEVER CONSIDER. RIGHT OR NOT.** BEAUTIFUL   CONSUME. WHAT ELSE?
(SELLING CARS) PREPARE.   PEOPLE.
                                               There's
always going to be a war.

an American. THERE IS A
PRESSURE. **AMERICA.** THE LINE BETWEEN SEX AND VIOLENCE AND POWER. The line between sex and violence and power. The unbearable pressure. The unbearable pressure. The unbearable pressure. Unbearable. The Pressure. The pressure. Unbearable. (The credits roll)
(Seen not represented) AMERICAN TELEVISION. AMERICAN TELEVISION.
(Now a word from your sponsor)
         (Somewhere between 120,000-38.000,000 died in the making of

Oppenhiemer (2023)) AND WHAT DOES IT MEAN TO HATE? AND WHAT DOES IT MEAN TO KILL? AND WHAT DOES IT MEAN TO HATE? AND WHAT DOES IT MEAN TO KILL?
AND WHAT DOES IT MEAN TO HATE? AND WHAT DOES IT MEAN TO KILL? AND WHAT DOES IT MEAN TO BE AMERICAN?

What do you do with the unbearable pressure? WHAT DO YOU DO WITH THE UNBEARABLE PRESSURE? What do you do with the unbearable pressure? **AND WHAT DOES IT MEAN TO HATE? AND WHAT DOES IT MEAN TO KILL?**

STAY TUNED. Fuck and hate and eat and kill. Fuck and hate and eat and kill. Filling the hole. Filling the hole. **There's nothing else**. Filling the hole. The pressure. Unbearable. The pressure. unbearable.AND THE HAMMERING. AND THE HAMMERING. The pressure. Unbearable. The unbearable pressure. The unbearable pressure. The unbearable pressure. **There's nothing else**. Repeating what they see and believing what they're told.
Repeating what they see and believing what they're told. **What do you do with the unbearable pressure?** Repeating what they see and believing what they're told. THIS IS YOUR BRAIN ON DRUGS. AND A LOT OF MESS.
Repeating what they see and believing what they're told. More holes. AND A LOT OF MESS.

AMERICAN TELEVISION. AMERICAN TELEVISION. AMERICAN TELEVISION. AMERICAN TELEVISION. What else?
Repeating what they see and believing what they're told.
THIS IS YOUR BRAIN ON DRUGS. (Now a word from your sponsor) A LOT OF MESS. PUT IT ALL TOGETHER. ONE PICTURE.

Beautiful people being beautiful
and sex/power/violence.
murdering and being murdered.
Never consider right or not. This is
not a full list RADICALIZED.

Filling in the hole. of side effects. More
holes. A LOT OF MESS.
AMERICAN TELEVISION. Just swallow.
Just swallow. NOW I AM BECOME
DEATH.

There's nothing else. Just swallow.
Over a billion severed (and
counting) There's nothing else.

BE PREPARED FOR BREAKING NEWS. ALWAYS
BREAKING NEWS.   COMBAT.
There is always going to be a war. WHAT ELSE?
Filling in the space. What Else? What else?
What else? What else?

There's nothing else.   (Now a word from your
sponsor)   AND WHAT DOES IT MEAN TO BE
AMERICAN?   AND WHAT DOES IT MEAN TO BE
AMERICAN?
A PRODUCT OF   CONSUME. CONSUME. WHAT
ELSE?   AND THE HAMMERING.
MY ENVIRONMENT. RADICALIZED. It's
almost unbearable. There's nothing else.
AMERICA. RADICALIZED. AMERICA. AMERICA
FUCKING AND HATING AND KILLING AND EATING AND
LAUGHING AND FALLING IN LOVE. AND THE
HAMMERING. AND THE HAMMERING. FUCKING AND
HATING AND KILLING AND EATING AND LAUGHING AND
FALLING IN LOVE. Alexander the Great wept. There's nothing
else. There's nothing else. There's nothing else.
There's nothing else. Being very scared. Being very
scared. Being very scared. There's nothing else.
FUCK WITH the LIGHTS off/KILL in PUBLIC
(SELLING INSURANCE) Being very scared.

There's nothing else.   A child.
A child.
                              HOW THEY BELIEVE. ALways
drilling and filling.
   THE LIGHTS OFF/ KILL   I AM A PRODUCT OF
MY ENVIRONMENT.

       IN PUBLIC   Always. Always.
ALways drilling and filling.
Always. THERE'S NOTHING ELSE.
CONSUME. ALWAYS. NOTHING ELSE.
ALWAYS. CONSUME. WHAT ELSE?
NOTHING ELSE? CONSUME.

                   How a child
repeats what
               they see and believe
               what they're told.
               A LOT OF MESS.   WHAT ELSE?
               CONSUME. WHAT ELSE? A LOT OF
               MESS. A LOT OF MESS AND
                         HATING AND
Consume. What else?   RADICALIZED. Hating and
killing.   THIS IS YOUR BRAIN ON DRUGS.
CONSUME.   RADICALIZED.

   RADICALIZED. AMERICAN TELEVISION. More holes.
THIS IS YOUR BRAIN ON DRUGS. AND THE
HAMMERING AND THE HAMMERING. AND THE
HAMMERING NEVER STOPS. THE HAMMERING
NEVER STOPS HAMMERING AND THE HAMMERING
NEVER STOPS.   CONSUME. CONSUME.

       AND WHAT DOES IT MEAN TO BE AMERICAN? AND
WHAT DOES IT MEAN TO LOVE? AND WHAT DOES IT MEAN TO
HATE? AND WHAT DOES IT MEAN TO KILL? AND WHAT DOES
IT MEAN TO FUCK? AND WHAT DOES IT MEAN TO EAT? AND
WHAT DOES IT MEAN TO BE AMERICAN?   CONSUME.
CONSUME.   WHAT ELSE? AMERICA. THERE'S

NO MORE WORLD LEFT. I AM A PRODUCT OF MY ENVIRONMENT. **A child. A child. Filling in a hole. A child.** (INTRO THEME PLAYS) (canned laughter) (A child screaming) A LOT OF MESS AND A LOT OF PRETENDING And the unanswered questions. IT's AMERICA. **A mess.** Confusion. AN UNBEARABLE PRESSURE. There's nothing else.

A child. Laughing at jokes he doesn't understand. A child.

American Television.

(NOW A WORD FROM OUR SPONSOR)

What it Means to be American,
a Personal Essay

I'm American   and I mean that. I'm
smiling. My father's a veteran   so
in my dreams   I'm an armored tank.
I watch a lot of television.
In America   on television   there's
a lot of strangers pretending to love
each other   and a lot of smiling.
I'm smiling   and I'm American   de-
spite having never fired a gun. In
America there are a lot of people fir-
ing guns   on television. In America
there's a lot of people pretending to
love each other. This is America   and
I'm smiling. My father is a veteran
despite having never fought in a war.
He is American   and he is my fa-
ther   despite having never taught
me how to fire a gun. I'm American
and I'm smiling   despite it meaning
nothing   and I mean that. When my
father was in the Army   they taught
him how to shoot airplanes down from
the ground   despite there being none
to   fire   at.   They were
pretending.
America is a lot of pretending.
America is a lot of smiling and   a
lot   of   firing   guns   but
nobody   smiles   when
firing   guns.
In America   when someone fires a gun
they   mean   it.
This is America.   I am American
and I am an armored tank.
This is America.   Everybody's
smiling.   Nobody means it.

America and the Truth

American children fill their summers
by catching fish   not to eat   to
amputate   a single fin   to leave
them swimming   in circles. We're
trying to diagnose the problem. We
dressed God like a cowboy   let him
drink all our beer. We murder our he-
roes and don't dream about the future.
In America everyone's a stranger.
We talk as if everyone's listening.
There's no more truth left to tell. We
want to die like our heroes. Fill our
days by thinking of all the different
ways We can kill Ourselves. We brace
ourselves for the End. We hate our
own mothers. We want to bury our fa-
thers. We have problems   undiagnosed.
We believe in other countries   only
in theory.   We let God drink all our
beer and drive home to His wife and
all His children. Our fish don't feel
pain. Our children amputate their fins
to watch them pretend to panic. In
America   we're swimming in circles.
God fell asleep behind the wheel. We
support the troops   only in theory.
We want to put bullets in the skulls
of our step fathers. The diagnosis
is bleak. Our heroes are dead. In
America   we're all suicidal and have
given up on God making it home safe-
ly. Everyone's a stranger and no one
is telling the truth. Brace yourself
for the End. In America   we're always
pretending   except when we're pan-
icking. Don't dream about the future.
There's no more truth left.

A Comprehensive History of Portsmouth, Ohio

It started with Henry Massie, 1803. Then there was a flood, 1937. Legend has it only one person died, a pregnant mother. They painted her dying breath on the murals in 1950. They say for every cockroach you see, there's a thousand you don't. A factory opened in 1902. It made shoelaces. April 3rd, 2013, Meagan Lancaster disappeared in a Rally's parking lot. She had a son. October 23, 2020, Mike Mearan was arrested on 18 charges, related to drug and human trafficking. They say for every cockroach you see, there are a thousand you don't. Some time in the mid to late 90s, the pill mills came in. In 2017, Billy Reinhardt died of an overdose. In 2019, so did Tesa Mcneely. They had two kids apiece. So far I'm counting 6. Legend has it there were so many overdoses in the summer of 2017 that they ran out of places to store the bodies. 350 people died in the flood of 1937, but they only painted one mural. By 2017, the shoelace factory, the one started in 1902, became a hub for sex workers. A local resident with a can of spray paint wrote "HIV/ HEP C, WE GOT IT HERE" on the building's crumbling brick. Documentaries were filmed and edited and broadcast on national television. In 2019 Dr. Margaret Temponeras was sentenced to 84 months for her role in distributing opioids to the surrounding area. Dr. Paul Volkman was given four consecutive life sentences. On October

26th, 2020, Mike Mearan pleaded not guilty. You know what they say about cockroaches. Bessie Tomlin. Meagan Lancaster. Billy Reinhardt. Tesa Mckeely. Between the four, they have six parentless children. In March of 2021, it was announced the shoelace factory, the one started in 1902, is being converted into a rehab. They covered the graffiti in white.

Sinkholes in America

November 1957. Russia launches a dog into space. Our infrastructure is crumbling. Moths don't batter their bodies against light bulbs because they like the sting. Roughly 3 billion years ago the first single cell organisms formed against all odds   at the bottom of the ocean. Humans will attempt to colonize Mars in my lifetime. The dog was never going to land. December 2021. Bridges are collapsing. Moths batter their bodies against light bulbs because their little insect brains beg them to find the moon   to stay out of the rain. December 1972. A sinkhole cracks open in the United States that's so big they give it a name. Roughly 3 billion years ago the first single cell organisms formed despite all the reason not to   at the bottom of the ocean. They had one purpose   survival. December 1967. A bridge collapses in Point Pleasant, West Virginia. They keep collapsing. The dog was never going to land. Roughly 3 billion years ago the first single cell organisms formed   just to die later   nameless   at the bottom of the ocean. Humans will attempt to colonize Mars in my lifetime. In all likelihood many of the participants will die before landing. Moths batter their bodies against light bulbs   hoping to stay out of the rain. November 1957. The dog is going to die soon and starts to panic the moment the rocket's doors are shut. November 1957. The rocket's doors are shut and they'll never open again. A bridge collapses in Point Pleasant, West Virginia. No saviors. December 1972. A sinkhole cracks open. They gave it a name. Roughly 3 bil-

lion years of infrastructure   crum-
bling. Humans will attempt to colo-
nize Mars in my lifetime. Survival
depends on it. December 2021. It's
raining and bridges are collapsing.
A moth's little insect brain begs it
to survive. November 1957. The dog is
going to die soon.

Theories on Car Wrecks and Other Forms of Suicide

Currently I'm working on several theories at once. There was a child in a car capable of speaking in complete sentences. It was snowing. I'm working on a theory explaining why some people put guns to their heads and why some of those people pull the triggers. The child was capable of speaking in complete sentences and had a basic understanding of the English language. His mother threatened to drive the car into the nearest building. The child had a basic understanding of the English language but couldn't understand his father besides the words *I wish you fucking would.*
I theorize that sometimes mothers drive into buildings attempting to save themselves. I theorize that people theorize when they're confused and terrified by something they don't understand. By theorizing they trick themselves into thinking they have some kind of control. They went to a video store. The snow became gray with dirt. To the child the girl behind the counter might as well have been God. I theorize that when children are confused and terrified they need every woman they see to be their mother. The child could speak in complete sentences. He heard his mother scream/ whisper *You ruin everything* to his father through her closed teeth. The child had a basic understanding of the English language but in that moment he wished he didn't. In between the family films and new releases was an aisle of pornography and recorded disasters. VHS tapes of bare

nipples. Buildings exploding and burning to the ground. Cars driving into buildings at top speed. A Santa Claus holding a pistol to his skull. I theorize people put guns to their heads for the same reason they theorize.

Me and Louie Anderson, Autumn of 1999

"Forgive your dad. He didn't mean it."
—Louie Anderson, 2018

It's the autumn of 1999. There is me and there is a television. I am a child and I am obsessed with a videotape of a movie that opens with a house and fades to black on a pile of smoldering ash. I never really watched the movie I don't know the title I just let it rewind so that the house miraculously pulls itself back together at the end. It's the autumn of 1999 and my father lies drunk on the front lawn and my mother is still sleeping on a mattress on the floor and now I'm watching a cartoon Louie Anderson play baseball while his father sits disappointed on the bleachers.   It's the autumn of 1999 and I am a child in a house that is slowly burning to the ground. It's the autumn of 1999 and there is me and there is a television   and everything else is black. It's the autumn 1999 and I am a child obsessed with a videotape that when rewound shows damage being undone and at some point in recent history an executive producer thought it would be a good idea to make a children's show that features an alcoholic father. It's autumn of 1999 and the sky is waiting patiently to be turned back to blue   and the thing I like the most about t.v shows is despite all disaster everything is back to normal by the end of the episodes I know that by the time the theme song plays cartoon Louie Anderson will be

unscaved   and no more truamitized
than usual. It's the autumn of 1999.
When the videotape I'm obsessed with
is nearly done rewinding   I see the
family unburned and very much alive
walking out of the front door   and
the mother is smiling, and the father
isn't soaking in Budweiser and uncon-
scious   and my father lies drunk
on the front lawn   and my mother is
still sleeping on a mattress on the
floor   and I am a child that is inca-
pable of putting out fires   and I am a
child that needs damage to be undone.
It's the autumn of 1999. There is me
and there is Louie Anderson. We're
both terrified by our fathers.

Matt Lauer, 2005/ Why I Learned to Stop Sleeping

In 2005 Matt Lauer in his infinite wisdom told me the world was ending sooner rather than later. It was a hot summer. My family was sharing bath water. The price of gasoline was too high and it had eaten a hole in the ozone layer. I was prescribed Adderall and told not to worry about how all our air was seeping out. I went to church. The preacher said that America isn't mentioned in the Bible for a reason. I was Baptized. I took my pills by mouth twice daily. When sharing bath water it's impossible to really get clean. Matt Lauer warned that bombs may drop on us while we dreamed.

A Beaten Dog/C-PTSD

Inflicting pain is always violent. And when an animal is stuck in that   in the violence   they develop a heightened urge to attack.   I am attacking as directly and effectively as I can. An injured animal won't explain itself. They aren't capable of it. There's almost nothing more natural. Violence in exchange for violence. An injured animal isn't capable of explaining itself. They shouldn't have to.

Everything Collected Turns to Rage

A prisoner. Left with no other chan-
nel to expel his rage   collects. His
shit and piss. Throws it at a guard.
This doesn't require thinking. The way
a dog snaps a rabbit's neck. The impor-
tance of survival to any lifeform. Like
a starving animal   a prisoner behaves
according to instinct. There's a part
of the brain that tells an animal when
it's being attacked and when it's in
danger. Necessary for survival. Left
with no other channel   a prisoner col-
lects. Shit and piss and the stink of
it. Mold and bacteria. Instincts tell
a lifeform to survive in its environ-
ment   any way it can. A prisoner and
his rage and nothing else. No way to
expel. An undesirable environment. An
animal trying to survive. No channels
for rage. Shit and piss is collected in
the body and later expelled. The way
the body does without thinking. A dog.
The neck of a rabbit. Rage. A prisoner.
Starving. An animal surviving any way
it can.

My Step Father Taught my Brother to Aim

An artist is born.   Shots   fired. A
plate of gunpowder. My brother wants
my step father dead. Art is supposed
to mean something. An artist designed
a gun.   If I had a bullet   I
would eat it. If I had a bullet   for
every time my brother wanted my step
father dead   I would have a full
stomach. Artists are people who make
statements. My brother ate plates of
gunpowder. My brother   is an artist
and an artist designed a gun   to
fire   and bullets to kill   and
if my brother had a bullet   and
if my brother had a gun   he would
make a statement.

Loneliness and the Resurgence of VHS Technologies

I predict   one day   videotapes of
beautiful people sleeping will be pro-
duced   marketed   and popularized in
the United States   and other industri-
alized countries   suffering from chron-
ic loneliness and correlated despair.
The sleepers' beauty   while appreci-
ated   won't be necessary. The impor-
tant part is that the viewer can hear
someone else's breathing. I saw this
in a dream   a few years ago.
I was   living   in Shelby's basement
was eating acid
like chewing gum   was less then
than I ever was   spent my time hid-
ing   daydreaming   about eating pussy
not because I missed the taste   but
because I wanted to be able to look up
and see someone   who's happy I'm
there   even if it's just for a moment
and I didn't care what she looked like
so long as she was alive   and I could
see the look on her face.

Norman Rockwell and a World That Never Existed

"We all know the atomic bomb is very dangerous. Since it may be used against us, we must get ready for it. Just as we are ready for other dangers that are around us, all the time. Now, you and I don't have a shell like Bert and Turtle, so we have to cover up our own ways. First, duck and cover."

> — Duck and Cover: Safety Instructionally Video, featuring Bert the Turtle, 1951.

Mom and Mary Ann and John Wayne. Apple pie. Uncle Sam. Jesus of Nazarus and Bert the Turtle and being lied to. Duck and cover. Stay low. Eyes closed. As painless as possible. The best attempt at survival. An atom bomb. A desk. Survival. The world is more complicated now. An apple Pie. Uncle Sam. A Cowboy. A gray diner at sundown. A showdown. A turkey dinner. Ugly children smiling. Norman Rockwell did his best to paint America. An airplane. An American Pilot. A lever pulled. Fat Man and Little Boy and Jesus of Nazarus of the United States of America. Sundown. Eyes closed. Little Boy and Fat Man and the horse they rode in on. A world that no longer exists. Mom. Mary Ann and Bert the Turtle and John Wayne. Apple pie. A young girl. A white gown. Crying in the mirror. Norman Rockwell paints the best he can. Adolf eats a fist of cyanide. The world is more complicated. A desk. The floor. The space in between. An atom bomb Detonated. Children. Duck and cover. The back of your head. Your face. Eyes. Ugly. There's less pain when lied to. Norman Rockwell doing the best he can. A gray diner. John Wayne. Not the killer clown. The Cowboy. America. A lie. Always a good guy and a bad. Always a showdown at dusk. America. Get down. Stay low. Put your head between your legs. Hold your breath. Closed eyes. The best attempt at survival ends with failing as painlessly as possible. Jesus of the United States and Bert the Turtle. Norman Rockwell did his best. World more complicated. A bomb. A desk. A turkey dinner and ugly children. There's less pain with eyes closed. A lie. America and John Wayne the killer cowboy. A rodeo clown. Adolf eats a bullet at dusk. Bert the Turtle dies for your sins. A girl in white. A turkey dinner. Ugly children. Crying in the mirror. Norman Rockwell did his best. A world that no longer exists. Never did. A lie. America. A rodeo clown. How we kill our heroes. Always a showdown at dusk. Always a good guy and a bad. Fat Man and Little Boy and Bert the Turtle and Norman Rockwell doing his best with America. A lie. More complicated. An atom bomb as painless as possible. A desk. A floor. The space between. Being lied to. Duck and cover. Closing our eyes. Like a turtle in its shell. Survival. More complicated now. Don't hold your breath.

Use Dynamite as Required

George Washington paid slaves for
their teeth. Alexander the Great wept.
The Catholic Church re-educated native
children. They even cut their hair.
George Washington had no problem chew-
ing steak. We carved our faces into a
mountain front. Used dynamite as re-
quired. The Catholic church cut Native
children's hair and buried their bod-
ies as Christians. There are no more
worlds left to conquer. The churches
are burning and I don't care. Slaves
were paid by George Washington for
their teeth as if they could have
said no. Native children were buried
as Christians in God's basement. Al-
exander the Great wept   and I don't
care   that the churches are burning.
I don't care that the churches are
burning. The churches are burning and
I don't care. George Washington ate
steak and there's no more world left.
The churches are burning. The churches
are all going to burn and I don't care.

The Stability/Instability
Paradox

In a car.   On   a   highway
going   no
s t o p p i n g   what so ever.
We are people who refuse to look at
other people. We are people   who I
can 't believe were ever children. In
America we think fish don't retain mem-
ory or feel pain   despite a lack of
evidence.
I theorize that engines bleed carbon
dioxide into cars   whether or not
there's a rag shoved in their tail
pipes.
On a highway   g o i n g   75   80
85.
We are people   who refuse to wreck
into each other.
On a highway   it's almost entirely
silent.
There's less war now than there's ever
been. No one wins in a car wreck. In
1 9 4 5   America dropped two bombs
and no one died exactly.   They just
stopped.   Even the people on the
highway refusing to look. On a highway
it's almost entirely silent
besides all the damn noise. There's
less war now than there's ever been. In
America we tell our children animals
don't know they're dying when killed
so it's easier for them to eat.
I theorize engines bleed carbon diox-
ide into cars   despite their best
efforts. I theroize there aren't any
children
not really. It's impossible
to remember a car wreck exactly as it
happened.   Impossible to pro-

cess or feel anything at all
in a fraction of a second   even
pain. Impossible
to realize the gravity of a bomb
dropping until after detonation
so the people who just stopped   who
were in cars   on a highway
in 1945   when America dropped two
bombs   didn't know the bombs dropped
didn't feel anything   not even
pain
so we have nothing to feel bad about.

Chris Watts Had a Problem

His wife was pregnant   again   and
he didn't love her. His daughters were
breathing. He had an oil tank. A truck
capable of hauling the bodies of sev-
eral former human beings
if necessary. Chris Watts is a man and
when a man has a problem he does what-
ever's necessary. It was necessary to
solve the problem. His wife was preg-
nant and his daughters were breathing
and he did not love. He had a truck.
He had an oil tank. He had two hands
capable of solving the problem   if
necessary. It was necessary to kill
his pregnant wife and the breathing
daughters he did not love enough to
keep alive/
to haul the bodies of the former human
beings to the oil tank in his truck/
to solve the problem.

Brenda Ann Spencer/ A Ruger 10/22, Semi Automatic

"I asked for a radio, and he bought me a gun."--Brenda Ann Spencer

Christmas day, 1978. A Ruger 10/22 semi automatic. Brenda Ann Spencer didn't like Mondays. Marsilio Ficino commissioned art. Brenda Ann Spencer's father bought her a gun. He taught her to aim. He taught her to aim. A cowboy fires a gun in the eardrum of Hollywood. Marsilio Ficino didn't really commission art. He was Ted Turner. He was Walt Disney. An artist designed a gun. They made Socrates drink Hemlock. Marsilio Ficino commissioned art of beautiful people being heroic. Brenda Ann Spencer's father bought her a gun. He bought her a gun and he taught her how to aim. He taught her how to aim. She taught herself to fire   like a cowboy. Eric Harris and Dylan Klebold killed 12 people. No one knows why. Hollywood makes their soldiers beautiful. Marsilio Ficino commissioned art. Marsilo commissioned cities. Socrates drank hemlock. Christ was nailed to the Cross. Christ was nailed to the Cross. Marsilio Ficino died and no one knows why. Brenda wanted a radio. Marsilio Ficino commissioned art of beautiful people. If a .22 caliber makes it through your body you won't feel pain. Christ was nailed to the cross and the nails went all the way through his body. Hollywood is deaf. Socrates drank hemlock and Morsilio Ficino commissioned cities. He was

Steven Spielberg. He was Charles Foster Kane. Christmas day, 1978. A Ruger 10/22 semi automatic. Brenda wanted a radio and hated Mondays. Marsilio Ficino wanted the soldiers to be beautiful. Cowboys fire guns. Christ was nailed to the cross and Marsilio Ficino made him look beautiful and so did Hollywood. Marsilio Ficino is dead. Brenda's father bought her a gun and she wanted a radio and he taught her how to aim and an artist designed a gun to fire. Brenda fired like a cowboy like a soldier. She fired and shot 11 people. No one knows why.

Short List of People I'm Trying to Kill

We're going to start with Martin Shkreli. That cunt bought the patent for a lifesaving drug   jacked up the price by hundreds of dollars a bottle   copped the only copy of the last Wu Tang Clan album with the cash. He won't let anyone listen to it. I want that fucking album and I want him fucking dead. And that's why I brought you all here. I have a plan. You're a very important part of that plan. This project is a collaboration.   I got it all sorted out. I need a plane ticket. I need a gun. A dish rag. A bottle of ether. I need a ride from the airport once I get where I'm going. I need a bag for the gun and the ether and the rag. I need a pack of adult diapers. I'll explain later. I need accomplices. I need fuckers who are down for the cause. These things are achievable but only through teamwork and dedication and elbow grease. I need teamwork and dedication and elbow grease.   I'm getting ahead of myself.   The second person I want to kill is Anish Kapoor. The cunt who made *the Bean* in Chicago. He owns the rights to the world's blackest paint and won't let anyone else use it. I'd like to drown him in that shit. And I mean really drown him. Get a barrel of it. Make him bob for apples until the bubbles stop popping. No apples. See how black that shit can get. That isn't cost effective though. Cash rules everything around us and whatever I use to kill with is going to be American made. I always buy American. American shit costs. I'll have kill as many birds with as few stones as possible. An artist has to be able to find freedom in their limitations. I'll have to line these fuckers up ear to ear to ear to ear. Put them on their knees.   Have you ever seen the movie *The House That Jack Built?*   I'll do it just like Jack did. But I won't fuck it up. I need a gun. A full metal jacket.   You have to buy American. I wrote that down on my forehead in permanent marker so I don't forget. I do it every morning and I wash it off in the shower every night. All capital letters. BUY AMERICAN. It's important to remember that violence is an art form and maybe the most honest of them all. A collaboration between victims and the artist and maybe the accomplices of that artist. The material does the work if you let it. It's exquisite. The tiger and the lamb and how they're both created by the same God and are perfect and necessary and so is art and so is violence and how art is violence and how violence is art and how it's all a collaboration.   Jim Irsay is the last cunt I'm going to kill. He bought the scroll Jack Kerouac typed *On The Road* on. AND WHAT GAVE HIM THE FUCKING RIGHT?   I'm sorry I'm screaming but I get excited when I know I'm right about something   and I'm really really right about something right now. I swear I'm not mad at you.   It's hard to define art. Some would say it's anything created. I would say it's anything created or destroyed. And some things need destroyed. If there's anything America can teach you it's that. It's important to remember that violence is the most American art form besides maybe Jazz and an artist has to work with the tools and materials they're comfortable with. The material does the work if you let it and that's why you have to BUY AMERICAN. ALWAYS BUY AMERICA. An artist designed a gun. It isn't enough to buy a synthesizer. You have to be able to play the fucking thing. If I can't paint with the blackest black I'll just find the next best thing. I need locations. Some rope would be nice. Some duct tape. Plane tickets. A gun. AN AMERICAN GUN. AN AMERICAN BULLET. A FULL METAL JACKET. A dish rag. A bottle of ether. A bag. Accomplices. People who are about this shit. People who are down for the cause. People who can drive. People with cars. With trunks big enough to store three living human bodies. People with gas money. I need a ride from the airport. A tank of oxygen. Enough to keep these three fuckers breathing awhile. We're taking a road trip to Chicogo. No piss breaks. We need a pack of adult diapers. When we get there I'll line them up ear to ear to ear to ear just like in that fucking movie. On their knees. In front of the Bean. One bullet. Three birds. An artist making a statement finding freedom with limitations. I'm going to learn to play the fucking thing. It's not enough to write a poem about killing these mother fuckers anymore. You have to get in the fucking car and go. We're going. That's final. No crying. THIS IS ART. CONTEXT. IT ISN'T MURDER IF THERE'S CONTEXT. THIS ISN'T A SATIRE. SATIRE'S FOR PUSSIES. THERE'S NOTHING FUNNY ABOUT THIS. I'M OUT

FOR BLOOD. I'M DOWN FOR THE CAUSE. I'M
ABOUT THIS SHIT. I need a gun a bullet
AN AMERICAN BULLET a full metal jacket
a plane ticket and a couple plane tick-
ets and accomplices and teamwork and
ether and a rag and elbow grease and
dedication and cars and drivers and
gasoline. ALL THIS SHIT COST FUCKING
MONEY. That's where you come in. Empty
your fucking pockets this is a God damn
robbery. This shit is American as fuck
and I'm proud to be an American and I'm
proud to be an American and I'm proud
to be an American and I need some fuck-
ing money if I'm going to make this
shit happen.

American Culture and its Consequences

Unicorns are mentioned in the Bible but America isn't. I'm an unmedicated bipolar. If I go to an automotive manufacturing plant   if I kiss a couple windshields with a baseball bat   I will be prosecuted to the fullest extent of the law. My views on gun laws have been radicalized. My views on everything. I'm unmedicated. America isn't mentioned in the Bible. We only talk about police brutality when we see footage of a man being murdered. American Culture has consequences. My views on everything have been radicalized. People admit to molesting their children on Dr. Phil. Fuck with the lights off. Kill in public. I'm an unmedicated bipolar. If I go to a gas station in Minford Ohio with $300   I can walk out with a gun. We hate junkies and feed kids Adderall for breakfast. If I go to an automotive manufacturing plant. If I kiss a couple windshields with a baseball bat. I might not make it out alive. America   and its consequences. I'm an unmedicated bipolar. If I walk into a gas station in Minford Ohio with $300   I can kill in public. In 2020 the NRA spent over $17,000,000 to influence gun policy in the United States. Oil companies spent over 300,000,000. To bust the Earth open like a windshield kissing a baseball bat. To suck it bonedry. I'm bipolar. I'm Unmedicated. I can maybe get $300. America isn't mentioned in the Bible for a reason. Culture has consequences. My views on everything have been radicalized. I think we should take all the guns. Start at the police stations.

Talk Shows and G.G. Allin's War on America, 1956-1993

1993. Only the strong survive. G.G. Allin's dressed for war. Says he's had sex with animals on stage and will do it again. Jerry Springer's hair isn't gray yet. August 1956. A child was born and named after Jesus. God is dead. 1993. G.G. Allin says his father was a violent man and that rape makes women stronger. John 14:6. Jesus says *I am the way the truth and the life*. January 1993. Bill Clinton becomes president. A child was born and now he's a man. Dresses in his shit. Says he drank his girlfriend's blood and went to prison for it. Says he burnt her with a blow torch. Says if it wasn't for rock and roll maybe he'd be a cult leader. Says he has our kids and we can't have them back. Says it's the parent's fault. Says he doesn't blame his father. Says he's the messiah. Says he's Elvis fucking Presley. Says only the strong survive. He spends a lot of time doing heroin and a lot of time dressed in his shit. He has a daughter and is a violent man. He befriends John Wayne Gacy and has him paint a portrait. Jesus dressed for war. 1993. G.G. Allin says when he throws his shit at people it's communion and he'll die in front of an audience. Says it isn't a cry for help. A lawyer on the Geraldo Rivera Show says what he does is illegal. 33 AD. Jesus is prosecuted to the fullest extent of the law. 1956. A child is born at war with America. He goes on Springer. Attempts genocide. Says he's going to bring down the government and weaponize the youth with rock and roll. Real rock and roll. Says he doesn't care whether or not you think it's art. 33 AD. Jesus dies in front of an audience. 1993. G.G. Allin's defending free speech on Geraldo. Says he plans to kill himself on stage. The audience applauds. Says you can't be a conformist. Says you have to do everything he says. John 14:6. 1933. Adolf starts a genocide. Says only the strong survive. 1993. John Wayne Gacy befriends G.G. Allin and paints a portrait. 1939. Adolf goes to war with the world. Compares himself to Christ. 1993. G.G. says he's daddy. Says he's God   Jesus and the Devil in one. Says he's Elvis fucking Presley. Says he fucks girls and boys and animals. Says he can't be stopped. Says if it wasn't for rock and roll maybe he'd be a serial killer. Says he's the answer. John 14:6. Says his daughter has to be strong. Says he's been angry since the day he was born. Geraldo asks if he had a troubled childhood. August 1956. A child was born. Named after Jesus. Became a prophet. He says he doesn't blame his father. 1993. A lawyer on Geraldo says there's distinctions between sex and violence. 1933. Adolf overthrows the government and says prison only made him stronger. 1993. G.G. Allin waves his hands like Adolf on Springer. John Wayne Gacy paints a portrait of Christ in a casket after a war. Jane Whitney is horrified. 1994. G.G. Allin didn't survive. 33 AD. Jesus dies in front of an audience. 1993. G.G. Allin wages war on Springer. He dresses like my father or someone he'd drink with. He says this isn't a uniform. Say this is how he dresses and this is how he smells.

When he goes home he cuts himself. Says he believes in rock and roll. Real rock and roll. Says he's just as invested in hurting himself as he is the audience. 1933. Adolf starts a genocide. 1993. A teenager takes the mic and stands firmly against censorship. G.G. Allin says rape makes women stronger. 1939. Adolf goes to war with the world. A lawyer on Geraldo says there's distinctions between sex and violence. 1956. A child is born named Jesus Christ. 1993. People argue about what art is on Geraldo while G.G. Allin brags about having sex with children as young as 12. Says he wants his daughter to be strong. Says he gets what he wants because he can take it. Says if it wasn't for rock and roll maybe he would've run for president. Says America worships a false God. Says he'd wipe his ass with the Bible. Says he was stabbed at a show once. Says he only makes enough money to post bail and go to the hospital. Says he was raped by the United States Judicial system. Says he spent a total of 3 years in prison and it only made him stronger. Says he's a human animal and he can't be stopped. Weaponize the youth. Overthrow the government. Real rock and roll. Die in front of an audience. He dresses in shit. Says he doesn't believe in compassion. Says *Bitch I can look you right in the eye. I am the only one who can teach you.* John 14:6. Jerry Springer tells him to clean up his language. God is dead. A lawyer on Geraldo says there's distinctions between sex and violence. *Because most people aren't turned on by violence.* 1945. Adolf dies in front of the world. 1993. G.G. Allin says he's going to kill himself and take our kids with him. His brother stands

up and says *it's a war out there.*
1994. G.G. Allin spent a lot of time
dressed in his shit and is dead now.
Said this is how I smell. John Wayne
Gacy painted a portrait. Christ in a
casket dressed for war.

Charlie Manson and Violence and the
United States' Prison Industrial
Complex and How They Correlate

How cancer cells form tumors. How if
you beat a dog long enough maybe it'll
learn to be loyal. How orphaned new-
borns can die from being unloved. How
Charlie needed a haircut. How the infra-
structure is crumbling. How dysfunction
breeds dysfunction. How we're products
of our environments. How the part of
the brain that tells an animal it's be-
ing attacked and when it's in danger is
necessary. How nothing prepares you for
combat but combat. How our fear is our
power. How there's going to be a war.
How Charlie said he did what he could
with what we threw away. How sea turtles
need to be able to fend for themself
from birth. How birds raised in labs
won't build nests for their eggs. How
children repeat whatever they see. How
they believe what they're told. How tu-
mors affect the body. How Charlie was
born in prison and died there. How he
asked an interviewer to imagine what
it'd be like to be interrogated by the
SS. How if you beat a dog long enough
maybe it'll learn to be quiet. How you
take someone's power. How it's 10pm do
you know where your children are? How
America has violence and drugs and what
they plan to do about it. How we lock up
and how we throw away keys. How a dog
chained to a dirt yard learns to lie in
the dirt. How caged rats will eat each
other. How at this rate one day there'll
be more of us in than out. How Charlie
said every man in prison is his father.
How a child repeats and believes what

they're told. How Charlie said he has
many children and we gave them to him.
How he asked an interviewer to imagine
what it'd be like to be interrogated
by the SS and what he meant when
he said it. How a beaten dog sharp-
ens its teeth. How nothing prepares
you for combat. How sea turtles learn
fear. How we lose our power. How can-
cer cells form tumors. How tumors af-
fect the body. How a dog chained to a
yard of dirt will learn to lie in the
dirt and for how long. How there's
always going to be a war. How America
has violence and drugs. How we lock
up. How we throw away. How a child re-
peats. How the part of the brain that
tells an animal it's being attacked
and when it's in danger is necessary.
How it's 10pm. How we don't know our
children. How dysfunction breeds dys-
function. How the infrastructure is
crumbling and what I mean when I say
that. More of us in than out. How if
you beat a dog long enough you'll see
what happens.

The Part of the Brain that Forms Society and The Part of the Brain That Designs and Sets Traps

"Humans are social creatures. We live in families, we work in teams, we envision duty and purpose through religious fellowship, we negotiate through economic alliances and political coalitions, and our norms are shaped by our cultures, itself an emergent property of group-living. Most of us probably take it for granted, as though it stood in no need of explanation or contemplation. But why do we live like this?"

    —Thoughts on the human's instinct to form
    society, Byran Parkhurst and Keith Tarvin

"Language is central to social interactions in all societies, regardless of location and time period. Language and social interactions have a reciprocal relationship: language shapes social interactions, social interactions shapes language."

    —Thoughts on language and society, Ashley
    Crossman

There's a city   someplace. And the people and the raw infrastructure. And all the organization that's required and the stink of organization. The reeking of it. The animal magnetism. The smell from something slowly breaking down. The language. Forged from an instinctual need to communicate and to be understood. How some things can't be communicated or understood. The word *culture*. The word *need*. The things the human brain is capable of and the things it isn't. The stacking of things

out of desperation. The running out
of space. The organization of lan-
guage and of people and the weapon-
ization of them. How everything that
can be weaponized has been or will
be. The horrible things the human
brain is capable of. The formation
of governing bodies. The weaponiza-
tion of organization and of fear.
Of uncertainty. The weaponization of
culture. In the reeking city full of
people and fear and stink and orga-
nization and stacking and stacking
and running out of space   there's
an alarming number of stray cats. The
word *alarming*. Designed to incite
panic. The way people organize people
around agendas. The word *agenda* and
the word *propaganda*. How they cor-
relate and their importance. Their
effect on the shape of a culture. The
word *culture*. Organized panic and
need and people and language for a
purpose. Weaponize. The word *weapon-
ize*. Weaponize fear and uncertainty
and words and the meaning of words.
The reeking of fear and uncertainty.
The reeking and the word *reeking*.
The rawness of it. The word *rawness*.
The infrastructure. The language we
forge out of the need to communi-
cate and how some things transcend
the need for communication. How the
urge to survive doesn't need to be
explained. How we don't ask why we
do it and why we don't ask why. The
rawness of *why*. The rawness of the
word *rawness*. The people and their
fears and their problems. The people
and their solutions. Their culture
and how norms are shaped. How the
human brain is capable of violence.

The natural inclination to design and set traps. The instinct to communicate and form society. The language and the fear. A People. A people weaponized. A weapon used against itself. The pointlessness of that and how painful it is to watch and be a part of. How *pain* isn't the right word for it. How pain transcends the word *pain*. Human violence and the rawness and the fear and the uncertainty. The stacking of people and the stink. The violence. The word *violence*. The word *need*. How they correlate. Something that transcends definition and how. When it's instinctual. In the organized city of reeking people weaponized the reeking weaponized people trapped coyotes. Starved them. Beat them. Sharpened their teeth by hand. Set them loose on the strays. How violence is never destroyed but transferred from one body to the next. The city the people the rawness reeking the word *reeking* the running out of space. The disorganization. The alarming amount of violence humans are capable of. The word *alarming*. The alarming violence of people and the people themselves and the peoples' needs. The people and their needs. And the stacking and the stacking. A culture of need. A people. Running out of space. Their problems. Their brains. Their language and their instincts. The solutions they're capable of and the violence. Their organization and weaponization and their language of rawness and their language of fear and their language of need. The words *fear* and *need* and *desperation* and *violence*. Their definitions and correlations. How long their definitions will matter and how long we'll have a need for words. The disorganization of people. The animal magnetism. How something transcends. How long before words become actions? The definition of the word *action*. The difference between the words *action* and *violence*. The word *need* and the word *violence*. The words *survival* and *violence*. How they correlate and how that doesn't need to be explained.

American Youth, The Early 21st Century

First the infants were born. Then the fathers suddenly consumed with confusion and already soaking in rage set fire to the houses. And the mothers exhausted and incapable of heroics let them burn. Then the infants watched television. Then the infants breast fed off Jerry Springer. And the fathers drank while the mothers dreamt suicide. Then the infants became children and the fathers acted psychotic and the mothers made the best of a bad situation. And the fathers kept drinking. And the fathers took narcotics. And the mothers did as they were told. Then children were taught to fear God to talk to Him without ceasing and the fathers demanded honor while the mothers prayed for miracles. And some of the fathers left and some of the fathers wanted to and some of the fathers stopped being fathers and some of the fathers never were and some of the fathers died and the mothers learned how to cry in silence and some of the fathers started setting fires again and some of them never stopped. And the fires kept burning. And the mothers kept breathing smokestacks. And the children coughed all night. And the fathers punched holes in the ceilings and the children ate the pieces by the palmful and the children's mouths held tablespoons of blood and the children were crucified for bleeding. And the children were no longer children. Then the teenagers stopped talking to God or fearing Him. Then the teenagers start-

ed drinking. Then the teenagers took
narcotics. And the teenagers wanted
to die and tried to. And some of
the fathers got sober and some of
the fathers found God and feared Him
and some of the fathers called the
teenagers psychotic and the mothers
incapable of heroics said nothing.
Then some of the teenagers became
fathers. And some of the teenagers
became mothers. And the mothers cru-
cified themselves for the infants.
Then the fathers with their bodies
smoldering and not even fearing God
stomped out fires   without ceasing.

A Hammering and the Hole it Made

there's satellites   everywhere
people   watch   beautiful people
people want   people want to be beau-
tiful   people never stop wanting
people never stop   never   people
used to do things   people used to
do a lot of things   for beauty
people   hammer jewels into teeth
remove skin   hammer out anything you
can   you can watch   beautiful
people   you can never stop   there
are more satellites than people   more
satellites than people
  the more people want the more they
watch   more people watching than ex-
pected   we're expecting satellites
to fall   remove sections of skeleton
remove unwanted skin   people want
less skin   people want more than
they are capable   unwanted people
want to be removed
people want to remove the people from
people   people want to remove the
people   because people are not
beautiful   people are people and
people never stop wanting   beautiful
satellites everywhere   and people
watching and wanting   and want-
ing never stops   the wanting never
stops   the wanting never stops   it
never stops   it never stops   the
wanting   it never stops people never
stop watching and wanting and it never
stops   never   people's wanting never
stops   unwanted people are people
and it never stops   the
hammering   the
satitles   are watching   the people
and there's a hole that the people try

not to talk about and the people are
not talking   and the hole is big
and the hole is impossible to ignore
and there's more than one   and the
people are full of holes   and the
people are watching the holes   and
digging   and digging   and digging
the people are watching the people
watching themselves talk to the peo-
ple who watch and who want and who
have a hole   who have more than one
and more all the time   and more all
the time   and more all the time
and it's more all the time   wanting
more   wanting more   want-
ing   more   hole   hole
hole   more   hole   more
hole   wanting   more   to be
hole   wanting to be more   hole
wanting   to be more   than   a
hole
and a hammering   and the hammering
never stops   hammering and the ham-
mering never stops   hammering   and
the hammering never stops.

The Suncoast Digest with Christine Chubbuck/Performance Art and American Television

"There's a pressure that comes with living in America. It's almost unbearable."

-Dan Denton, 2022

"In keeping with the WXLT practices in presenting the most immediate and complete report on local blood and guts news, TV 40 presents what is believed to be a television first, in living color, an attempted suicide."

—Christine Chubbuck, on Suncoast Digest, July, 1974, right before the bullet fired.

"An artist designed a gun to kill."

-A fact about the nature of firearms

"We suffer at our sense of loss. We are frightened by her rage. We are guilty in the face of her rejection. We are hurt by her choice of isolation and we are confused by her message."

-Minister Thomas Beason, eulogy of Christine Chubbuck

"People fire guns to make statements."

-A fact about the nature of people

"TV 40 news personality Christine Chubbuck shot herself in a live broadcast this morning on a Channel 40 talk program. She was rushed to Sarasota Memorial Hospital, where she remains in critical condition."

-Christine Chubbuck, a prediction of her own suicide, written before she pulled the trigger

"An artist makes a statement, at any cost. Even when we don't understand."

—A truth about the nature of artists

Blood and guts and in living color. Bullets and guns and American television. The bedroom of a teenage girl. An artist with a message. Christine had a problem communicating. *If it bleeds it leads,* her producers say. She read the news. There's a pressure. America. A sense of loss. Confusion. The face of rejection. She bought a gun. Blood and guts. Rage. A bullet. An artist. She put on puppet shows in her spare time. Confusion. The room of a teenage girl. A virgin. Unbearable. Frightened. An artist with a problem communicating. Loneliness. A pressure. Blood and guts and guns and bullets and our sense of loss. Things that America understands. The choice to isolate. Rejection. America. Guns. Designed to kill. The confusion of a teenage girl in the face of America. Christine. An Artist. A television first. Critical condition. America. *If it bleeds it leads.* An overdose in the early 70's and a gun bought a week before being fired. A sick joke/A cry for help/A prediction of suicide/A problem communicating. An unbearable pressure. America. A puppet show. A frightened artist with a problem and a message and a bullet and a gun. Blood. Guts. Confusion. Rage. A statement. Something that America understands.

American Television and Unanswered Questions

What do you get when the Ouroboros
keeps eating? And what do you get when
you buy your daughter a gun? And what
do you do when your father's a veter-
an? And what do we do about the crum-
bling infrastructure? And what do you
do about the burning churches? And what
if the hammering doesn't stop? And what
do you do when you don't have a chan-
nel for your rage? And what do you get
when you beat a dog? And what do you do
when you can't put out the fire? What
if nothing's painless? And what is the
meaning of pain? And what do you get
when you drill holes in a child's head?
And what does the tiger want with the
lamb? And what do you do when you've
become comfortable with your mess? And
what do you do when you're a man with
a problem? And what do you do when you
kill your wife and children? And what
else was God going to do with the bod-
ies? And what do you do when a poet
lies to you? And what do you do with
a .22 caliber? And why won't the ham-
mering stop? And what do you do when
eating leaves you hungry? And what do
you do when you kill what you love? And
what do you do when it hurts to swal-
low? And what do you do with the un-
bearable pressure? And what do you do
when the bombs drop while you're sleep-
ing? And what do you do when they teach
you to shoot at airplanes? And what do
you do with the body of Christ? And
what do you do with all the blood? And
what do you do when rape doesn't make
you stronger? And what is the distinc-

tion between sex and violence? And why do we kill in public? And why did Alexander weep? And why did Marsilo glorify war? And what do we do with all our soldiers? And what do we do with all these strays? And what do you do when you have questions without answers? And why is the world so complicated? And what if the rocket never lands? And what do you do when swallowing is no longer an option? And what did Gacy do with the bodies? And why did Socrates drink the hemlock? And what did Norman Rockwell do with America? And how many bodies are buried in God's basement? And what did Brenda do with her gun? And what did Chris do to his family? And why do we fuck with the lights off? And what is the distinction between sex and violence? And what do you do with the blood and the guts? And what do you do when your house is on fire? And what do you do when you don't love? And what do you do when you don't know your children? And will we ever stop swimming in circles? And what do you do with all your confusion? And what do you do with your loneliness? And what do you get when you hate what you fuck and love what you kill? And what do you do with the unbearable pressure? And what do you do with the unbearable pressure? And what if everything blurs together? And what if the rocket never lands? And what do you do with the unbearable pressure? And what if it all starts to repeat? And what if there's no world left? What do you do when the poems stop making sense? And what do you get when Americans stop smiling? And what's it like to be interrogated by the SS? And what do you do when they throw you away? And what do you get when you beat a dog too long? And what if the rocket never lands? And what do we do when the infrastructure crumbles? And what do we do with all the cockroaches? And what do you do when you're not busy coping? And what do you do when your head's very busy? And what do you do when you have a problem communicating? And what do you do when fucking is violent? And what is the distinction between love and hate? And what do we have to feel bad about? And where are the martyrs? And what do you get when a problem goes undiagnosed? And what do you do when given a gun? And why did an artist design them? And why are you pointing it to your head? And what do you do when it all feels like a prison? And what do you do when the dog bites back? And why do we kill in public? And what do you do when you're an armored tank? And what do you do when the airplane finally hits the ground? And why were you shooting at it to start with? And why do we fuck with the lights off? And what is the definition of the word survival? And what does it actually mean? And what does the tiger do with the lamb? And why is the world so complicated? And why isn't America mentioned in the Bible? And what if we'll always be running circles. And what do you do when you're a child in America? And what do you do when there's no one left to shoot at? And what do you do when there isn't any truth left? And what do you do when it stops making sense? And what do you do with all your confusion? And what do you do with American television? And what do you do when there's only vomit? And how do you trap a coyote? And what if you can't find the meaning? And what if there's nothing left worth dying for? And what did your daughter do with the gun? And what if the rocket never lands? And what do you do when being American means nothing? And what if there's no world left? And what happens when the Ouroboros runs out of shit to eat? And what do you do with the un-bearable pressure? And what do you do with the unbearable pressure? And what do you do with the unbearable pressure? And what do you do with the unbearable pressure? And what do you do with the unbearable pressure? And what do you do with the unbearable pressure? And what do you do with the unbearable pressure? And what do you do with the unbearable pressure? And what do you do with the unbearable pressure? And what do you do with the unbearable pressure? And what do you do with the unbearable pressure? And what do you do when you can't answer these questions?

J.I.B. is a prose poet and essayist from Southern Ohio. His work has been published with journals, magazines, and various Midwest presses. You can follow his work, travels, and performances on instagram @j.i.b.trash.poet or on Facebook @ J Ian Bush.

This project was made possible, in part, by generous
support from the Osage Arts Community.

Osage Arts Community provides temporary time, space
and support for the creation of new artistic works in a
retreat format, serving creative people of all kinds —
visual artists, composers, poets, fiction and nonfiction
writers. Located on a 152-acre farm in an isolated rural
mountainside setting in Central Missouri and bordered
by ¾ of a mile of the Gasconade River, OAC provides
residencies to those working alone, as well as welcoming
collaborative teams, offering living space and workspace
in a country environment to emerging and mid-career
artists. For more information, visit us at www.osageac.org

Osage Arts Community

www.ingramcontent.com/pod-product-compliance
Lightning Source LLC
Chambersburg PA
CBHW041151120626
46547CB00020B/3181